Really *WILD*

DOLPHINS

Claire Robinson

First published in Great Britain by Heinemann Library,
Halley Court, Jordan Hill, Oxford OX2 8EJ,
a division of Reed Educational and Professional Publishing Ltd.

Heinemann is a registered trademark of Reed Educational & Professional Publishing Limited.

OXFORD MELBOURNE AUCKLAND
JOHANNESBURG BLANTYRE GABORONE
IBADAN PORTSMOUTH NH (USA) CHICAGO

Designed by Celia Floyd
Illustrations by Alan Fraser (Pennant Illustration)
Printed and bound in Hong Kong/China by South China Printing Co.

03 02 01 00 99
10 9 8 7 6 5 4 3 2 1

ISBN 0 431 02872 9

British Library Cataloguing in Publication Data

Robinson, Claire
Dolphin. – (Really wild)
1. Dolphins – Juvenile literature
I. Title
599.5'3

Look at the dolphin at the bottom of each page. Flick the pages and see what happens!

Acknowledgements
The Publishers would like to thank the following for permission to reproduce photographs: Ardea London Ltd: Francois Gohier p.4 (left), 11, 12, 17, 18; BBC Natural History Unit: Jeff Foott p.4 (right), Hans Christoph Kappel p.5 (right), Jeff Rotman pp.6, 10, 16, 20, 22, Kit Rogers p.9; Environmental Images: Paul Glendell p.19, Robin Culley p.21; FLPA: Leatherwood/Earthviews p.5 (left), Marineland pp.14, 15; NHPA: Norbert Wu p.13; Oxford Scientific Films: Hans Reinhard p.7, Alan G Nelson p.23. Bruce Coleman Limited: Jeff Foott Productions pp.8-9;

Cover photograph: Oxford Scientific Films/Konrad Wothe.

Every effort has been made to contact copyright holders of any material reproduced in this book. Any omissions will be rectified in subsequent printings if notice is given to the Publisher.

Contents

Some words are shown in bold, **like this**. You can find out what they mean by looking in the glossary.

Dolphin relatives

Dolphins are sea **mammals**. Their close relatives are whales and porpoises. There are over 40 different kinds of dolphin. Here are some of them.

bottlenose dolphin

spotted dolphin

dusky dolphin

killer whale

Killer whales are the largest dolphins. A dusky dolphin is one of the smallest. This book is about bottlenose dolphins.

Where do dolphins live?

Some bottlenose dolphins live in the Atlantic Ocean, some live in the Pacific Ocean, and others live in the Red Sea. They are never too far from land.

Dolphins live in large groups called
schools. They **protect** their babies from
sharks and look after each other.

Moving around

Dolphins are good swimmers. They can stay under water for several minutes. They swim by moving their tails up and down. Flippers help them twist and turn.

8

Can you see the hole on the top of the dolphin's head? It breathes air through this **blowhole** as it leaps in and out of the water.

Communicating

Dolphins can find their way using sound. They make clicking noises in air passages under their **blowholes**. Sounds come out through the round part of their heads.

If there is a rock or boat ahead, the sound bounces back as an **echo**. Dolphins also **communicate** with each other with squeaks, whistles and moans.

Finding food

Dolphins travel together to search for fish and **squid**. They swim around a **shoal** of fish to stop them escaping.

Sometimes the dolphins hit the fish with their tails or **stun** them with loud sounds. The fish cannot move and they are gobbled up.

Babies

This female is giving birth. Her baby is born tail first. The mother pushes her baby up to the **surface** to breathe.

The young dolphin stays close to his mother. He will drink milk from her teats for over a year.

Growing up

This young dolphin has learnt how to hunt. Look at her teeth. They are the right shape for catching this fast, slippery **squid**.

Young dolphins stay close to their mother for several years. When she has taught them enough, they join other young dolphins in the **school**.

Playing

Dolphins are very **intelligent** animals.
They enjoy playing, too – just like us.
These two bottlenose dolphins are
leaping in the air.

Sometimes dolphins ride on the **bow** waves made by the movement of a boat through the water. This is fun and is less tiring than swimming.

Dolphins and people

Bottlenose dolphins seem to enjoy being near people, as long as people are gentle with them. This one has met a diver.

But sometimes dolphins are in danger from people. This baby got caught in a fishing net and drowned. Some dolphins are also caught for food.

Dolphin facts

- There are sometimes many hundreds of dolphins in a **school**.

- A baby dolphin is about 1 metre (3 feet) long. Adults can grow up to 3.7 metres (12 feet).

- Dolphins have very smooth, silky skin which helps them swim fast.

- Dolphins are in danger from the nets used to catch tuna fish. You can help save dolphins. Read the label on the tin to make sure the tuna you eat was not caught in nets that are dangerous to dolphins.

- Sometimes bottlenoses swim together with other kinds of dolphin and whales.

Glossary

blowhole   a hole on top of a dolphin's head, used for breathing

bow   the front of a boat

communicate   to give others information and let them know what you think and feel

echo   a sound that bounces back

intelligent   clever

mammals   a warm-blooded animal that feeds its babies on milk, some mammals have hair

protect   keep safe

school   a group of dolphins

shoal   a big group of fish

squid   a sea animal with eight trailing arms

stun   to shock

surface   the top of something, in this case the sea

Index